CHASE

A POLICE STORY

BY ALISON HART
with the assistance of
the Staunton, Virginia, Police Department

photographs by Dennis Sutton

RANDOM HOUSE 🏠 NEW YORK

The author and editors would like to thank
the police and civilian personnel
of the Staunton, Virginia, Police Department
for their assistance
in the preparation of this book.
Special thanks to Officer Kevin Pultz,
forensic photographer.

Library of Congress Cataloging-in-Publication Data
Hart, Alison. Chase : a police story / by Alison Hart ;
with the assistance of the Staunton, Virginia, Police Department ;
photographs by Dennis Sutton.— 1st ed.
p. cm. SUMMARY: A police officer must use her best judgment
while trying to catch an escaped convict who has stolen a car
and is headed for Staunton, Virginia.
Audience: Grades 2–5. Audience: Ages 7–10.
ISBN 0-679-89367-9 (pbk.) — ISBN 0-679-99367-3 (lib. bdg.)
[1. Police—Fiction. 2. Staunton (Va.) Police Dept.—Fiction.]
I. Sutton, Dennis, ill. II. Staunton (Va.) Police Dept. III. Title.
PZ7.H256272 Pu 2002 [Fic]—dc21 99-054079
Printed in the United States of America First Edition May 2002
10 9 8 7 6 5 4 3 2 1
RANDOM HOUSE and colophon are registered trademarks of
Random House, Inc.

Please note: Words printed in **boldface** are defined in the glossary at the back of the book.

1700 HOURS

5:00 P.M.   The blue sedan zips past the police car hidden behind the overgrown shrubs on the shoulder of Route 11. Officer Amy Collins checks her radar display. The sedan's going sixty miles an hour. Fifteen miles over the speed limit.

Officer Collins flips the switch to turn on the blue bar light on the roof of her police car. She pulls out from behind the bushes and onto the road.

RADAR

Officers are trained to use radar to check the speed of moving vehicles. There are two parts to a radar unit. The antenna is mounted outside the rear window of the police car. The display unit is mounted on the dashboard. The unit uses sound waves to track how fast a vehicle is moving.

The speed in miles per hour flashes on the digital display in bright red numbers.

COMMUNICATIONS CONSOLE/CAR RADIO

One of the most important pieces of equipment in the police car is the radio, which is mounted on the communications console. On the police radio, officers can talk as well as listen. They press a button to "key" the mike when they want to talk.

The Staunton Police Department has its own radio frequency. No one else can broadcast on that frequency. The police  car's radio is on all the time, but unless someone is talking, it is quiet.

Officers need to be in constant communication with the dispatchers in the 911 Center. The dispatchers are their source of help in case they get in trouble. And the dispatchers give them important information, such as the location of a traffic accident or robbery.

CODES

All police officers use codes when talking over the radio. The Staunton Police Department uses the Ten Codes, which make it easier for police to communicate quickly. For example, **10-38** means "traffic stop." **10-50** means "accident."

Each officer also has his or her own badge number. Officer Collins is **6-6**. Her shift commander, Sergeant Harlow, is **2-5**.

As she heads after the sedan, she picks up her radio mike. She calls the **dispatcher** at the Staunton Police Department: "Staunton, 6-6. 10-38. Virginia license ARC58W. Ingleside and Route 11."

The sedan pulls over to the side of the road. Officer Collins stops a car length behind. She parks so she can easily see the driver's-side door on the sedan. As she climbs from her police car, she turns on her portable radio.

LICENSE PLATE

Every car on the road must have a license plate. The dispatcher uses a teletype machine to run the number on a plate through the Department of Motor Vehicles (DMV). The DMV automatically does a "wanted check" on the license plate through the National Criminal Information Center (NCIC) and the Virginia Criminal Information Network (VCIN). The wanted check will tell the officer whether the car is stolen or has been used in a crime.

PORTABLE RADIO

When police officers get out of their police cars, they switch on their portable radios, or "walkies." Most officers use a walkie with a shoulder mike. The speaker is worn on the shoulder epaulet of the uniform, close to the officer's ear, so he or she won't miss important information. This arrange-

ment also enables the officer to speak into the mike while keeping both hands free.

Leaving the car running, she walks to the sedan. The driver rolls down the window. A woman with gray hair peers nervously up at her. "What's wrong, Officer?"

"Ma'am, may I have your license and **registration**, please?" Collins asks politely.

"But why?" the lady asks as she digs through her purse.

After she's handed over the license and registration, Officer Collins replies, "You were traveling sixty in a forty-five-mile-an-hour zone."

"Sixty!" the woman exclaims. "I couldn't have been going *that* fast!"

"I clocked it on radar, ma'am."
Collins checks the photo on the
license. It matches the woman's face.

DRIVER'S LICENSE

Every driver of a car must have a license. All Virginia driver's licenses have a photo. The officer always checks to make sure the photo matches the driver. The number on a license can be run through the Department of Motor Vehicles. Information received will tell the officer whether the license is valid and whether there are any restrictions—for example, if the driver must wear glasses.

If the driver looks or acts suspicious, the officer can decide to run a wanted check on the driver's license. This will show whether the driver has committed a crime in another area.

She walks back to the police car, careful to avoid traffic. Climbing in, she keys, or turns on, her mike. "Staunton, 6-6. Run a check on Virginia driver's license 1855799."

While Collins fills in the traffic **summons sheet**, she continually glances up at the blue sedan. For the past five years, in the United States, at least one of every three police officers killed in the line of duty was killed while making routine traffic stops.

Collins knows she has to stay alert.

1705 HOURS

5:05 P.M. Sitting in the 911 Center of the Staunton Police Department, dispatcher Janice Burke hears a state trooper calling on the SIRS radio. She hits the SIRS select button and says, "This is Staunton Police Department."

"Staunton, this is State Unit 7575. We have a report that an **inmate** escaped from a **prison work crew** on Interstate 81 and stole a green Chevy from the rest area at Weyer's Cave.

SIRS

SIRS (Statewide Interdepartmental Radio System) is a special radio channel that allows all the officers in the state of Virginia to talk to each other. No codes are used. If a crime happens outside the city of Staunton, the Staunton dispatchers will hear it over SIRS. They may then radio the information to the Staunton officers, if necessary.

He forcibly removed the driver from the vehicle. He was last seen exiting the interstate at Weyer's Cave ten minutes ago. Unknown direction of travel. Inmate is a white male wearing a blue work shirt, blue jeans, and work shoes."

As Janice listens, she writes down

every word on a yellow legal pad. The 911 Center receives three hundred to five hundred calls in every twenty-four-hour period. This one is especially important. Weyer's Cave is only ten miles from Staunton. The escaped inmate could be heading into the city.

Janice **acknowledges** the message. Immediately, she selects the police **frequency** and hits the red alert tone. "Staunton, all units. Be on the lookout for—"

1710 HOURS

5:10 P.M. "—an escaped inmate . . ."
Officer Collins stops filling out the
summons to listen to the car radio. "The
escapee has **carjacked** a green Chevy,
Virginia license WEF47X."

Collins pulls her daily record pad
from the visor and jots down the
license number. It's been a long, slow
shift, but after she listens to the
message, her interest picks up. If the
inmate has exited at Weyer's Cave,

DAILY RECORD PAD

Police officers often take notes while on duty. Many use a daily record pad to jot down anything suspicious or unusual. For example, an officer may write down the license

plate number of a car parked by a store late at night. If by chance that store is robbed, the license number could be useful in finding the robber.

Other officers may write down the license number of every car they stop, or notes about every person that they talk to while on duty. That way, if something happens to the officer, there is a record of the last person he or she had contact with.

he could be traveling south on Route 11—right toward Collins.

As Collins continues filling in the summons, the loud whoosh of a speeding vehicle catches her attention. She glances up as a green car flies past. Collins figures it has to be moving close to eighty miles an hour. Automatically, her gaze locks on the license plate. "WEF—" Before she can read the rest of the plate, the car disappears into the southbound traffic.

The three letters match the license of the stolen car. The stolen *green* car.

Throwing the clipboard on the seat, Collins jumps from her car. She rushes over to the blue sedan.

"You're free to go, ma'am," she says as she quickly passes the woman her license and registration. "Consider it your lucky day."

Collins hurries back to her car, slams the door, and reaches for the mike. As she pulls into traffic, she radios dispatch: "Staunton, 6-6. I believe the stolen vehicle you gave the **BOL** on just passed me. I am attempting to catch up to it. We're heading south toward the intersection of Route 11 and 275."

Blue light flashing, Collins weaves around several cars until she's behind

the green Chevy. Keying her mike, she reads off the entire license plate. The dispatcher radios back, "Yes, that is the stolen vehicle."

PURSUIT POLICY

All police departments have very strict rules about chasing fleeing vehicles. The rules are meant to keep officers and civilian drivers safe. Only in very serious cases can officers drive through red lights or stop signs, and they must slow down and carefully check to make sure no other cars are coming. They can drive faster than the speed limit, but they cannot be reckless. If there is a lot of traffic or roads are slippery, police officers must slow down. Officers must also wear seat belts at all times.

Only police vehicles that have a siren and a blue light may be involved in a pursuit. The siren and lights are turned on to warn other drivers.

The light turns red. The Chevy cuts in front of a pickup truck. The truck swerves into Collins's path. She slams on the brakes.

Ignoring the light, the Chevy barrels through the intersection. Tires squeal as a bread truck screeches to a halt to avoid hitting the fleeing car.

Collins turns on the siren. "Subject just ran the red light at Route 11 and 275," she tells dispatch, her heart racing. "I am in **pursuit**!"

1715 HOURS

5:15 P.M. Sergeant Mark Harlow swiftly exits the back door of the Staunton Police Department and heads for his police unit. As he climbs into the four-wheel-drive Explorer, he hears dispatch over the radio. "Staunton, all units, 6-6 is in pursuit of the stolen vehicle. Hold all **non-emergency calls**."

Five minutes ago, Harlow was sitting at his desk writing up a monthly report. He's in charge of the day shift and his main duty is supervising six officers, which requires a lot of paper-

CODE A CALL

Dispatchers often decide the importance of calls they receive. They assign a "priority" code to determine how fast the officers should respond.

A Code A call is urgent. A robbery, riot, bomb threat, or serious accident would be a Code A.

Officers can assign a Code A priority to a pursuit if they feel the situation is life-threatening or if they are dealing with a fleeing criminal. They can then initiate emergency vehicle operations. This means they use lights and sirens and can bend certain traffic rules. A shift commander can end a pursuit at any time.

work. A Code A call changes all that.

"Staunton, 2-5. I'm en route," Harlow says as he backs the vehicle around. "See if you can get some units headed that way."

"2-5, be advised that no units are available at this time."

As Harlow pulls from the parking lot, he mentally runs through the list of available officers on duty. Fry is processing an arrest at the jail. Davenport is tied up on a **domestic call**. Whitmore is finishing up a shoplifting report at Wal-Mart. Larner is on bike patrol in the park. Corporal Doyle is on vacation.

"2-5. 5-6," he radios Officer Jason Whitmore. "How soon before you're free?"

"Be about a minute."

"As soon as you can, proceed up Coalter to assist Officer Collins."

Harlow realizes that right now he's the closest officer on duty. He needs to get to Collins fast. His officer needs **backup**.

Harlow pulls onto Lewis Street, blue light flashing, siren blaring. Again he hears Collins on the radio: "Staunton, 6-6. I'm behind the vehicle heading south on Augusta at this time. The speed is about seventy-five miles

per hour. There is a single driver."

Harlow curses the traffic as he heads up Lewis Street. Cars pull over sluggishly when they hear him coming.

CHASE

As he approaches a red light, he slows and checks for oncoming cars before speeding through it. No matter how urgent the call, Harlow knows he has to drive safely. He has to arrive alive if he's going to assist Collins.

1715 HOURS

5:15 P.M.   Officer Collins grips the steering wheel as the police car careens around the corner. She tries to keep the green Chevy in sight, knowing how quickly a fleeing vehicle can disappear.

As she drives, questions whirl through her mind.

Where is the inmate headed? Does he have a weapon? Can I catch up to him without causing an accident? Where's my backup?

Collins glances at the radar unit secured on the dash. The escapee's going almost *eighty* miles per hour. The speed limit is thirty-five. Up ahead, the road splits—Augusta Street veers to the right, Coalter to the left. Either road leads into crowded downtown Staunton.

At the Y intersection, the Chevy zooms toward the right. Collins keys her mike. By now, Harlow should be traveling north on Augusta. Collins hopes the sergeant will **intercept** the fleeing vehicle.

"Staunton, the subject's heading south on—"

Without warning, the Chevy cuts sharply to the left, trying to make the turn onto Coalter Street. The brakes lock, and the car slides sideways. Gravel flies as the tires scream against the pavement.

Ka-boom! The car smashes into a telephone pole at the point of the Y. Dust goes flying and a street sign thunders to the ground.

The crash is so sudden, Collins drops her mike.

Stomping on the brakes, she forces the police car to a screeching halt.

The Chevy's right side is wrapped around the telephone pole. The hood's popped open and steam hisses from the engine. The driver is slumped over the steering wheel.

In a split second, Collins makes several decisions based on her training and experience. She parks the police car so it's not too close to the Chevy. The crashed vehicle could easily catch on fire. She also positions her car so the traffic on both roads won't run into the wreck. She keeps the blue lights on for warning, then quickly calls dispatch for help.

Without backup, Collins does not rush over to the car. The inmate may be faking injury. He may have a weapon.

POLICE TRAINING

Staunton Police Officers are highly trained.

Basic Training: In Staunton, police **recruits** go through fourteen weeks of basic training. Firearms, crime investigation, and defensive driving are a few of the classes they might take.

Field Training: The new officer works alongside an experienced police officer for twelve to fourteen weeks. The last two weeks, the new officer is in charge. The experienced officer supervises.

Routine Training: Each officer must have forty hours of training every two years to keep current. The officer might take classes in fingerprinting or use of firearms.

Specialized Training: This is extra training. Officers may take these classes to learn a new skill or become better at what they do. These could be classes about school violence, first aid, or accident investigation.

CHASE

Collins keeps her eyes trained on the Chevy while she talks. "Staunton, 6-6. Subject has just wrecked at Augusta and Coalter. He may be injured. Get fire and rescue—*whoa!*"

The Chevy's door flies open. The inmate jumps out and races across Coalter Street.

Collins throws open the car door and shouts into her mike, *"Subject has bailed out of vehicle and is running toward Oakbrook. I'm on foot pursuit!"*

1720 HOURS

5:20 P.M. As Sergeant Harlow listens to Collins on the radio, he grips the steering wheel tighter. An escaped convict—loose in a neighborhood—is a dangerous situation. The guy could grab a hostage, carjack another vehicle, or barricade himself in a house. Harlow might need to activate **CIRT** or call for **canine**.

As he speeds north on Augusta, Harlow keys his mike. "Staunton, 2-5.

Notify Captain Dickerson of the situation."

The captain will have gone home for the day, but department policy requires Harlow to contact his superior officer. Captain Dickerson will then contact Chief Wells. The captain and chief need to be kept informed. Still, Harlow's the one who will make the decisions. It's his responsibility to make sure nothing goes wrong.

POLICE/RESCUE/FIRE INTERACTIONS

One of the dispatcher's jobs is coordinating services between the police department, the fire department, and the rescue squad (who are trained for medical emergencies). When a police officer is on a scene, he or she can't communicate with fire and rescue through the police radio. The officer depends on the dispatcher to contact them.

At a serious accident, the fire department and rescue squad are usually called to the scene along with the police. Each department knows its job. Fire makes sure the vehicle doesn't ignite and also cleans up any hazardous spills. Rescue checks people for injuries and transports them to the hospital, if necessary. Police are in command of the situation, direct traffic, and write up the accident report.

1725 HOURS

5:25 P.M. "Staunton, all units. 6-6 is in foot pursuit of an escaped convict on Oakbrook," Janice radios from the 911 Center. She's sitting tensely in the chair, nervously twirling her pen. The second dispatcher on duty is handling all the other calls. Janice needs to focus totally on Collins's situation.

Janice **tones** the firehouse. "Engine 3 and Engine 5. Responding. This is a fire alarm. We need to have you **stage** at the accident scene on Coalter and Augusta and assist in traffic control. We are still in pursuit of the subject. The scene is not **secure**."

Next she calls the Staunton-Augusta Rescue Squad. She has already contacted State Unit 7575 and advised him that one of the Staunton officers was following the stolen vehicle.

When she's through, Janice takes a quick sip of Pepsi. It's been several minutes since Collins's last contact. *Where is she? Is she okay?*

Janice would love to call into the mike, *"Collins! Are you okay?"* but she knows she must keep the frequency free in case the officer tries to contact her.

She glances up at the map of Staunton. Oakbrook Road winds

around a wooded area with many houses and several side streets. The inmate could disappear in an instant.

Janice tries to guess where the two are headed. If an officer gets in trouble, she has to know where to send help.

Collins's life is in her hands.

1730 HOURS

5:30 P.M. Officer Collins streaks across the church parking lot. She picks up speed, trying to keep the inmate in sight. She doesn't want to lose him.

The escapee leaps down a hill, disappearing for a moment. Then Collins sees him run into someone's front yard. Without slowing, Collins dashes across the parking lot and down the hill, sliding in the dirt. The inmate crosses the yard, then heads around toward the back of the house.

Breathing heavily, Collins runs to the back corner of the house. She stops, then has a quick peek around just in time to see the inmate run behind the house next door. Collins sprints through the front yard to the house next door, edges along the side wall, and peers around the corner. She scans the backyard, checking out the flower beds, brick patio, two lounge chairs, grill, and air conditioner unit.

The subject is nowhere in sight.

But then Collins spots an odd shadow—as if someone is hiding behind the air conditioner. Ducking behind the corner, she keys her shoulder mike. "Staunton, the subject is in the backyard of the second house on the left on Oakbrook."

Fire and rescue sirens sound from Coalter. *Where are Harlow and Whitmore?*

Collins is pretty sure the inmate's holed up behind the air conditioner. But the guy could run any second. She decides not to wait for backup. Collins draws her gun from the security holster.

Crouching, Collins moves around the corner, gun in the low-barricade

position. *"Police officer!"* she hollers, jumping up. *"I see you behind the air conditioner. Come out with your hands up. I need to see your hands!"*

1735 HOURS

5:35 P.M. *Collins is at the second house on the left on Oakbrook.* Janice grabs the city directory. Heart pounding, she skims the pages, quickly locating the address. She calls the house number over the radio to all the responding units so they can locate Collins.

Then she phones the owners of the house. A woman finally answers after the fifth ring.

CITY DIRECTORY

The 911 dispatchers must locate information quickly. One way is to use a city directory. It has four sections.

Alphabetical Section: This is like a regular phone book. Last names are listed in alphabetical order.

Business Directory: This is like the Yellow Pages. It lists businesses, stores, restaurants, etc.

Telephone Key, or "Reverse Directory": In this section, the dispatcher uses a phone number to find a person's name and address.

Street Guide: Dispatchers use this section the most. In it, they can look up an address to find a person's name and phone number. For example, an officer may call and say, *"I'm at 489 Troy Street. There is a broken window. There may have been a burglary. Can you tell me who lives here?"*

"Mrs. Smith, this is Staunton Police Department dispatcher Burke," Janice says calmly, though she is feeling anything but calm. "We have an escaped suspect at large around your residence. For your safety, *lock your doors* and stay in your home. We will call you when we have any further information."

"Staunton, 5-6," Jason Whitmore calls in. "I'm on Coalter, approaching Oakbrook. Responding to backup."

Thank goodness. Janice twirls her headset cord, her stomach still churning. Any minute, Harlow and Whitmore should be at the scene. She hopes Collins will wait for them.

1735 HOURS

5:35 P.M. Sergeant Harlow turns onto Mountainview, slowing long enough to check out the wreck at Coalter and Augusta. Since the Staunton-Augusta Rescue Squad is located on Coalter Street, two ambulances are already parked at the wreck site. The **emergency medical technicians** will wait in case someone is injured during the pursuit.

The fire truck has pulled into the

church parking lot. Firefighters dressed in bright yellow protective suits mill around the wreck. They've set up flares. Two firefighters are directing traffic.

Harlow notes that the situation is under control. He turns left onto Coalter, then takes a sharp right on Oakbrook. The second house. He's got to find Collins.

1735 HOURS

5:35 P.M. Collins aims her gun at the air conditioner. The shadow doesn't move. "Show me your hands," she repeats. "Come out from behind the air conditioner. You're under **arrest**."

Collins's voice is steady even though she knows what a dangerous spot she's in. The inmate is desperate. He's carjacked a vehicle and run from a prison work crew. That means a lot more jail time. He has nothing to gain

LOW-BARRICADE POSITION

The officer crouches and holds his or her gun low and in both hands. This position makes an officer a three-foot target instead of an approximately six-foot target. And if someone tries to grab the gun, it's easier for the officer to pull back and get away or shoot in self-defense.

by giving up without a fight.

"Hands in the air!" Collins hollers.

Slowly, one arm rises into view.

"Now the other one!"

The left hand sticks up—then, in a blur of movement, the inmate dashes from behind the air conditioner and races across the patio.

Holstering her gun, Collins takes off after him. As Collins runs, she shouts into her mike, "Staunton, subject's heading for the woods behind the house."

Collins leaps over a lounge chair, then sprints across the lawn. The inmate's only fifty feet ahead, but he's heading up the hill toward the woods behind the house.

Only one thing is on Collins's mind— catching the guy. If she loses the inmate in the woods, the odds of capturing him are slim. And if the guy carjacks another vehicle or grabs a hostage, someone could get hurt.

This may be Collins's last chance.

1737 HOURS

5:37 P.M. Sergeant Harlow screeches to a halt and parks in front of the second house on the left of Oakbrook. He doesn't see Collins or the escapee.

He climbs from his police car, one hand on the mike. "Staunton, 2-5. Attempt to contact 6-6."

He hears dispatch call Collins twice. There's no response.

Frustrated and worried, Harlow whacks the roof of his Explorer.

"Staunton, 2-5. As soon as 5-6 arrives, we'll search the area."

A second later, a police unit races up and parks behind Harlow. "Where's Collins?" calls Officer Whitmore as he jumps from his car.

"Somewhere behind the house," Harlow says, already striding across the front lawn. "Go around the left side. I'll go right. Stay parallel to me as we travel across the backyard to the woods. And stay in sight."

As Harlow jogs around the house, he unsnaps his security holster. He has no idea what he's getting into—and he wants to be ready.

SECURITY HOLSTER

The security holster is designed so that only the person wearing it can easily remove the gun from the holster. Staunton officers carry their weapons

in *break-front* holsters. The officer must move the gun forward and out to remove it. This prevents a criminal from pulling the gun out from behind or from the side and using it against the officer.

1740 HOURS

5:40 P.M. Collins's lungs are ready to burst as she scrambles through a flower bed. She's closing in on the escaped inmate. Slowing just a second, the convict glances at the cop over his shoulder.

That's all Collins needs. She lunges. Shoving the guy in the shoulders, Collins sends him sprawling. She dives on top, landing with her knees square in the man's back. Instantly,

Collins sticks her left knee against the inmate's neck and grabs for the guy's arms.

The inmate struggles to get away, jabbing at Collins with his elbows. Collins catches a wrist and twists it. The inmate screams, but it's a scream of rage, not pain.

With her free hand, Collins reaches behind for her cuffs. "Give me your other hand!" she orders.

The guy yanks his left arm out of reach. "I'm not going back!"

Collins twists the captured wrist harder. "Bring your arm around. Do it *now.*"

USE OF FORCE

Police officers are trained to use only the amount of force necessary to arrest someone. An example of minimum force is putting handcuffs on someone. An example of maximum force is shooting someone. Deadly force is when someone is killed.

Maximum force is used by officers only when it is *absolutely necessary* to protect themselves or others from serious injury or death. In the last fourteen years, no Staunton police officer has had to use deadly force.

The escapee drags his left arm around to his back. Collins snaps the cuffs around both wrists. Quickly,

she runs her hands down the inmate's
body, checking for weapons.

Still kneeling on the man's back,

HANDCUFFS

All officers carry handcuffs in pouches on their gun belts. Handcuffs are used to ensure the safety of the arrested person, the officer, and possibly others. Officers may choose to handcuff a person's hands in front of his or her body or in back.

Collins breathes deeply, trying to slow her pounding heart. Then she keys her mike. "Staunton, 6-6. Subject's **in custody**."

1743 HOURS

5:43 P.M. Cheers erupt in dispatch. *"Way to go, Collins!"* Janice whoops. Then she quickly gets back to business. "Staunton, all units. 6-6 has the suspect in custody at this time."

She calls the State Department of Corrections and State Unit 7575 and tells them that the inmate has been captured. Next, she contacts rescue. Someone may be hurt, and it's Janice's responsibility to see that *everybody,* even the criminal, is taken care of.

"Rescue 57, the suspect is in custody at this time. Please respond to the
second house on Oakbrook to check
for minor injuries from the accident.
The scene is secure."

1745 HOURS

5:45 P.M. Harlow jogs toward Collins at the same time Whitmore comes around the other side of the house. "You okay?" Harlow calls to Collins.

Collins nods, and Harlow blows out a breath of relief. Not only is he responsible for his officers, he cares about them, too.

"Man, Collins," Whitmore says with a smile. "What took you so long to catch the guy?"

Collins grins. Sweat rolls down her forehead. She looks beat.

Harlow glances over at the prisoner. He looks just as beat. His face is streaked with dirt, and there's a fresh red scrape on his forehead from the accident.

But no one was seriously hurt. No property was damaged. And the escapee was caught.

"What do you need?" Harlow asks Collins.

"My car's back at the accident," Collins replies as the officers escort the inmate around the house to the street. "I'm going to need transport."

"Have the EMTs check the prisoner over, then put him in Whitmore's vehicle," Harlow tells her. "I'll drop you off at your car and you can follow them in."

Both officers nod.

"When Davenport shows up," Harlow continues, "I'll get him to work the wreck. You have enough to do."

Sergeant Harlow knows how much work a car accident involves. It is the officer's job to take photos of the scene, get the vehicle towed, make sure the street's cleaned up, draw a diagram of the scene, interview witnesses, and write up an accident report.

TRANSPORT

Persons who are arrested are transported in the back seat of a police car. There are no door handles in the back of a police car. These back doors can only be opened from the outside. They lock automatically.

A wire screen and Plexiglas shield separate the front and back seats. The screen keeps the arrested person from touching or grabbing the officer in front. The shield protects the officer from being spat on.

Harlow jerks his head toward the inmate. "After the EMTs check this guy over, get him out of here."

1800 HOURS

6:00 P.M. Back at the police department, Collins climbs from her car. Officer Whitmore has pulled in front of her. Collins can see the suspect in the back of Whitmore's car.

"You want me to go in with you?" Whitmore asks as he pops the locks on his car doors.

"Yeah. Hang out for a minute, too, so I can get the forms I need."

Collins and Whitmore flank the

inmate as they walk him through the back entrance and into the **processing room**.

"Have a seat." Collins nods to a plastic chair. The inmate plops down, a bored expression on his face.

"I need your name and date of birth. I know you've been fingerprinted before, but we need a new set. And I've got to photograph you."

The inmate eyes her. "What're you charging me with?"

"To start with, reckless driving, eluding a police officer." Collins puts ink on the fingerprint pad and rolls the ink out. "But hey, that's nothing.

FINGERPRINTS/PHOTOS

Anytime a person is arrested, he or she must be fingerprinted and photographed. Fingerprints can change slightly over time. A person might have a new scar or an injury on the pad of a finger.

A new photograph is especially important since a person's appearance can change dramatically—for example, because of a new haircut or hair color, new eyeglasses, altered facial hair, or simply the process of growing older.

You've got to worry about the state. They're going to charge you with the prison escape *and* carjacking."

"Then why don't you drop your charges?" the guy asks. "The escape's going to add enough years to my jail time."

Collins shrugs. "Should've thought about that before you took off."

The inmate's shoulders slump. His fight is gone. The chase is over. He was caught, and he knows he's headed back to prison.

"Okay, now let's get your cuffs off and get these fingerprints done," Collins tells him. "I'm sure you're dying to get back home to jail."

Officer Larner, who's also on Collins's squad, sticks his head around the door. "Hey, Amy, I heard you had a slow afternoon," he jokes.

By now, everybody at the police department knows what happened. Later, when the prisoner is gone, most of the officers will stop by to hear about the chase and joke about it. Retelling the details of a tough arrest often helps an officer deal with it.

"Yeah. Yeah." Collins waves Larner away. Her mind's on all the paperwork she's got to complete: a pursuit report, an offense report, a use-of-force report,

OFFICER'S DAILY REPORT

OFFICER _____ DATE _____ SHIFT/UNIT _____ HOURS _____

ARRESTS

FELONY _____
MISD. _____
JUV. _____
DUI _____
OTHER _____

SPD Form 11-25-81-21

TRAFFIC SUMMONS

HAZARDOUS _____
NON-HAZARDOUS _____

ACCIDENTS INVESTIGATED

FATAL/P.I. _____
OTHER REPORTABLE _____
NON-REPORTABLE _____

OFFICER _____ BADGE NO. _____

UNIT NO. _____ DATE _____

VEHICLE REPAIRS NEEDED: _____

ENDING MILEAGE _____
OIL USED _____ QTS _____
TIRES REPLACED # _____

ISSUED BY: _____

SPD Form 2-14-83-48   EQUIPMENT CONTROL CARD

OFFICER'S DAILY REPORT

When officers first go on duty, they are briefed, or told, about important things that happened during the prior shift. They might be given the description of a missing person. Or they might be told to BOL (*be on the lookout*) for a stolen car. Officers enter this information onto their daily report forms. At the end of their shift, they add additional information such as how many arrests they made and/or how many tickets they gave out. This report goes to the shift commander before they leave.

three summonses, and the daily report.

Her shift is over by seven, but she'll be lucky if she's home by nine.

Only thirty minutes went by from the time Officer Collins spotted the stolen Chevy to the time she cuffed the inmate.

A thirty-minute rush. Two hours of paperwork.

That's police work.

GLOSSARY

acknowledge—to let someone know that you have heard what he or she has said. *When the dispatcher wants the officer to know she has received his message, she says, "10-4." That is the Ten Code for "acknowledged."*

arrest—to take to jail or court. *The police officer will arrest the robber.*

backup—officers called to a scene to

help a fellow officer. *When she sees the situation is dangerous, Officer Collins calls for backup.*

BOL—short for "be on the lookout." *The dispatcher sends a BOL over the radio.*

canine—the police unit that works with police dogs. *Officer Harris is a canine officer. He works with Kally, a police dog.*

carjack—to take a vehicle (car, truck, van) by force. *After the man pulled the* *woman from the passenger seat, he carjacked her vehicle.*

CIRT—Critical Incident Response Team. CIRT officers are trained to use special weapons, such as submachine guns. They are trained to work together as a team to deal with dangerous situations. *Sergeant Harlow will call out CIRT if the inmate barricades himself in a house.*

dispatcher—a person who handles the calls in a 911 Center. *The dispatcher received an urgent call from a store about a robbery.*

domestic call—a fight or argument that involves family members. *The officer went to the house in response to a domestic call.*

emergency medical technician (EMT)—a trained medical professional who helps sick or injured people until they arrive at the hospital. *The EMT checked the young man's blood pressure.*

frequency—a particular portion of the radio spectrum. *Different radio stations use different frequencies so their signals won't get mixed up.*

in custody—in the care of the police. *The inmate is now in custody.*

inmate—a person who's living in a prison. *The inmates staged a riot because they didn't like the food.*

intercept—to catch or stop on the way. *The officer intercepts the robber before he escapes from the store.*

non-emergency call—any type of call to a dispatcher that does not need an immediate response. *The phone call about the barking dog was a non-emergency call.*

prison work crew—inmates who have earned the right to work outside the prison may be on a work crew. Sometimes they receive pay. *The inmates on the prison work crew picked up trash along the highway.*

processing room—the place where a person who has been arrested goes to have his or her fingerprints and photo taken. *In the processing room, the officer took a photo of the suspect.*

pursuit—a chase. *The officer is in pursuit of the car thief.*

recruit—a new member of a police force who has not gone through training. *The recruits would have to pass fourteen weeks of training before they could wear police uniforms.*

registration—a legal document showing who a car belongs to. *My mother's name is on the car registration.*

secure—to make safe. *The officer will secure the building after the robbery.*

stage—to set up and prepare an action. *The officers will stage behind the bank.*

summons sheet—a written form that the police officer fills in and gives to any person who has broken the law. It is a promise to appear in court on a certain date and time. The person must sign it. *The officer gave a summons sheet to the woman who was caught speeding.*

tone—when the 911 dispatcher alerts the firehouse or rescue squad about an emergency. It causes an alarm to go off and sets off the firefighters' and EMTs' pagers. *The dispatcher tones the rescue squad so they can quickly respond to the car accident.*

Don't miss

RESCUE

A POLICE STORY

by Alison Hart
Written with the assistance of
the Staunton, Virginia,
Police Department

When a shrill beep alerts 911 dispatcher Cyndi Deaver-Seay to a holdup
at Painters Bank, she isn't worried. The
Staunton police get about a hundred
false alarms each month.

Nevertheless, per normal procedure, Cyndi sends two police units to
make contact with the bank. But the

bank's not following normal procedure today. And what's about to happen is anything *but* normal.

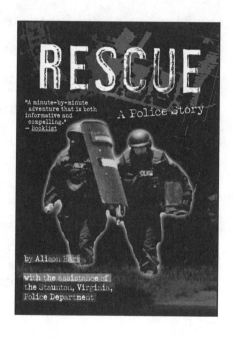

ISBN: 0-679-89366-0

ABOUT THE AUTHOR

ALISON HART is the author of over sixty books for young people, among them the Edgar Award–nominated middle-grade mystery novel *Shadow Horse*. Because she loves mysteries and true crime, working with the Staunton Police Department was a dream come true. Ms. Hart has a master's degree in communicative disorders from Johns Hopkins University and is a graduate of the Staunton Citizens' Police Academy. She teaches creative writing and developmental English at Blue Ridge Community College. Ms. Hart lives in Mount Sidney, Virginia, with her husband, two kids, three cats, a dog, and two horses.

About the Photographer

Up until 1995, when he retired after a thirty-six-year career, **DENNIS SUTTON** was the chief photographer for the Staunton *Daily News Leader.* In the years before photography became a function of police officers, Mr. Sutton did most of the crime photography for the Staunton Police Department, the Augusta County Sheriff's Department, and the Staunton area office of the Virginia state police. For many years, he was also an active member of the Staunton reserve police. Mr. Sutton has received numerous awards from the Virginia Press Association, and his photos have appeared in *Newsweek, People,* and the *Washington Post.* He lives in Vesuvius, Virginia.